Spot the Difference

# Noses

Daniel Nunn

Heinemann Library
Chicago, Illinois

Customer Service   888–454–2279

Visit our website at www.heinemannlibrary.com

Photo research by Erica Newbery
Designed by Jo Hinton-Malivoire
Printed and bound in China by South China Printing Company
10 09 08 07 06
10 9 8 7 6 5 4 3 2 1

**Library of Congress Cataloging-in-Publication Data**
Nunn, Daniel.
  Noses / Daniel Nunn.
    p. cm. — (Spot the difference)
  Includes bibliographical references and index.
  ISBN 1-4034-8476-7 (hc) — ISBN 1-4034-8481-3 (pb)
  1.  Nose—Juvenile literature.  I. Title. II. Series.
  QL947.N86 2007
  599.14′4—dc22

                          2006007244


**Acknowledgments**
The author and publisher are grateful to the following for permission to reproduce copyright material:
Alamy p. **6** (Steve Bloom); Ardea pp. **7** (Ingrid van den Berg), **19** (M.Watson); Corbis pp. **8** (Zefa/Daniel Boschung), **11** (Yann Arthus-Bertrand), **14** (Tim Davis), **18** (Royalty Free), **21**; FLPA p. **5** (David Hosking); Getty Images pp. **17** (Gallo Images/Martin Harvey), **20** Blend Images); Nature Picture Library pp. **4** (Aflo), **9** (Jose Schell), **10** (Andrew Harrington), **13** (Lynn M. Stone), **16** (Gertrud & Helmut Denzau); NHPA p. **12** (Jany Sauvanet); Science Photo Library p. **15** (Gary Meszaros).

Cover image of a cow's nose reproduced with permission of Alamy/Ace Stock Limited.

# Contents

# What Is a Nose?

nose

Many animals have a nose.

Animals use their nose to smell.

Animals use their nose to breathe air.

Most animals have their nose on their head.

# Different Shapes and Sizes

Noses come in many shapes.
Noses come in many sizes.

This is a moose.
It has a big nose.

This is a mouse.
It has a small nose.

This is an anteater.
It has a long nose.

This is a cat.
It has a short nose.

This is a pig.
It has a flat nose.

# Amazing Noses

This is a monkey.
It has a red and blue nose.

This is a mole.
It uses its nose to find its way.

This is a camel.
It can close its nose.
This keeps out sand.

trunk

This is an elephant.
It uses its nose to pick up things.

This is a polar bear.
It can smell food from far away.

This is a dog.
It uses its nose to find things.

# Noses and You

People have noses, too.

People use their noses to smell.
People use their noses to breathe air.
People are like other animals.

# Spot the Difference!

How many differences can you see?

# Picture Glossary

 **breathe** take in air

 **smell** sense something using your nose

# Index

**Note to Parents and Teachers**

National science standards recommend that young children understand that animals have different parts that serve distinct functions. In *Noses*, children are introduced to noses and how they are used to smell and breathe. The text and photographs allow children to recognize and compare how noses can be alike and different across a diverse group of animals, including humans.

The text has been carefully chosen with the advice of a literacy expert to enable beginning readers' success while reading independently or with moderate support. An animal expert was consulted to provide both interesting and accurate content.

You can support children's nonfiction literacy skills by helping them to use the table of contents, headings, picture glossary, and index.